How to Cope with
DANGEROUS SEA LIFE

A Guide to Animals that Sting, Bite,
or are Poisonous to Eat from the Waters of
the Western Atlantic, Caribbean, and Gulf of Mexico

Edwin S. Iversen
Renate H. Skinner

Windward Publishing, Inc.
105 NE 25th St.   P.O. Box 371005   Miami, Fl. 33137

Copyright © 1977 Windward Publishing, Inc.

ISBN 0-89317-017-8
Library of Congress No. 77-81166
3 5 7 9 10 8 6 4
Printed in the United States of America

Table of Contents

Foreword 4
Introduction 4
Chapter 1.   Animals That Bite 6
Chapter 2.   Animals That Sting 12
Chapter 3.   Animals That Are Dangerous to Eat 22
    Poisonous Animals 22
    Animals Containing Pollutants 36
    Diseased and Parasitized Animals 40
    Non-parasitic Diseases of Fish and Shellfish 43
Chapter 4.   Some Other Pests: Red Tide, Erysepeloid
            Bacteria and "Swimmers Itch" 53
Chapter 5.   Guidelines 55
    How to Avoid Endangering Your Health 55
    Rules to Follow if Bitten, Stung or Poisoned 56
    Treating Stings, Wounds and Bites 56
Detailed Symptoms of Fish Poisoning 57
Sources of Information On Dangerous Sea Life in Florida and
    Adjacent Waters – Research Institutions and Libraries 58
References 61
Index 63

Foreword

Southern waters support extensive commercial and recreational fisheries that are rapidly increasing in intensity as the human population grows, along with the associated greater increases in water use: fishing, diving and bathing. The substantial expenditures associated with sport fishing, boating and scuba diving are a valuable asset to the economy of this area.

Our overall objective in this book is to impart knowledge about potential harm from stinging, biting or poisonous marine organisms and the ways known to deal with any problems which might develop so that bathers, boaters, divers, fishermen and seafood lovers may find greater enjoyment of the bountiful sea and beautiful beaches in this part of the world. This is not a "scare" book. It is not our intention to frighten people about dangerous sea life!

For those of you who desire, or require, more specific information, we provide references for further reading (page 61), as well as the names of organizations and libraries which can provide additional information (page 58).

We are grateful to Dr. Donald P. deSylva and Robert C. Work, University of Miami, RSMAS, for their useful criticisms of the manuscript. Thanks go to Warren Zeiller and Jim LaTourrette, Miami Seaquarium, Dr. John E. Randall, Bernice P. Bishop Museum, Hawaii, and Frederick H. Berry, NMFS, Southeast Fisheries Center, for kindly providing photographs used herein, and to Jane Iversen for illustrations and editing services.

Introduction

In this guide we describe some of the potential dangers from certain marine life found in the warm seas of the southern Atlantic coastline of the United States, the Gulf of Mexico, the Caribbean, the Bahamas, the West Indies and Mexico. Some of the creatures are unfamiliar, others may be familiar; some of them bite, some sting; others are diseased or parasitized which may cause you to wonder if they are edible; some contain poisons such as ciguatera or have unhealthy levels of pollutants like heavy metals or pesticides which may make them unsafe to eat.

We answer here many questions that arise every day about these creatures, providing accurate and recent information about dangerous sea life. In addition we suggest how to avoid situations where you might be stung or bitten, and the means of safeguarding your health by proper preparation of your catch for eating. Information on the effects of eating fish and shellfish from polluted areas is included.

If you are bitten, stung, or become poisoned, we provide suggestions on first aid that has been found successful, until you can get professional help. *In all cases, if you are seriously injured by one of these animals, seek medical attention!*

Although books have become available in the past decade about dangerous sea life from around the world, they are rather general; that is, they contain less useful, specific information about a particular location. No new book on poisonous or harmful sea life in this area has been published since "Sea Pests: Poisonous or Harmful Sea Life of Florida and the West Indies," written by C. Phillips and W. H. Brady in 1953 (now out of print). Our guide, "How to Cope with Dangerous Sea Life," provides similar and additional up-to-date information.

Some organisms are harmful to man by nature or because of pollution by man. All marine organisms are subject to disease, infection and infestation by parasites. When commercial fishermen, fish processors and recreational fishermen find fish parasites or diseased fish, they generally want to know about the parasite or disease and whether the fish is suitable for human food.

Over the years we have answered hundreds of questions of this sort by phone and letter at the University of Miami. Inquiries are increasing, in part at least in response to the greater fishing intensity. While inquiries come largely from sport and commercial fishermen, physicians occasionally inquire as to the role marine parasites play in human disease. Considerable knowledge of poisonous fishes, fish parasites, and stinging and biting sea life and their role in human health can be found in technical journals, but is not easily available to those who need and seek it.

Many cases of poisonous fish and shellfish have been recorded from tropical locations other than the southern United States, the Gulf of Mexico, the West Indies and the Bahamas. For some families of poisonous fishes we have no valid records that they have caused human sickness or death in these waters, but since fishes in these families are poisonous elsewhere, they are presumed to be poisonous here. Therefore, we have included them in this guide.

It is important to note that the mere lack of authentic records does not of itself mean that a marine species or individuals of a species are safe to handle or eat, for the following reasons:
1. The relationship between eating poisonous marine organisms and the illness is not always recognized.
2. Identification of the sea life that caused the illness was incorrect.
3. Illness caused by marine animals is frequently not reported to health authorities.

Although this volume is written primarily for the southern United States, the Gulf of Mexico, the Bahamas, and the West Indies, it has value elsewhere in tropical and subtropical marine waters because hazardous fish and shellfish are there also, usually with different common and scientific names, and the safety and prevention principles are the same.

Some people scoff at the notion that some animals are poisonous because in their experience around the water they have never been troubled by these animals. This simply points up the normal variations in susceptibility and response of humans to poisons. Furthermore, a person's age also affects his response to poisons. In this book an animal is considered dangerous if any cases of poisoning, stinging, or biting have been authentically recorded.

The size and age of the animal can also affect its danger to man. For instance, barracudas tend to be more poisonous when they are large. Shellfish that have been exposed to man's pollution for extended periods tend to accumulate more toxic chemicals and when eaten are more dangerous to man.

Also, some animals may be dangerous for more than one reason; for example, they may bite and also their flesh may be poisonous to eat. The barracuda, shark and moray fit this category; therefore, they are discussed under two chapters in this guide. The species in the chapters are listed in alphabetical order.

We were unable to obtain photographs of a few of the dangerous species listed in this book. In such cases we have used a photograph of a very similar and closely related species.

Chapter 1.
Animals That Bite

There are many books filled with information on "savage" marine animals, especially sharks. Recent popular books and films on shark attacks and the habits of sharks have increased public awareness of the problem. In many beach resorts considerable economic depression can result when shark attacks are sensationalized. One popular beach on the east coast of Florida has averaged two shark attacks per year over the last 20 years, some of which have received nationwide attention in newspapers and on television. The accounts, written in a sensational manner, do not consider the number of bathers using the beaches year round. When viewed from this standpoint of numbers, one can see that the chance of being bitten by a shark is very small. Nonetheless, shark attacks are a very serious problem, especially if you happen to be a victim.

Sharks will not ordinarily attack humans, but like any large wild animal, their behavior is unpredictable and occasionally they can be very dangerous. Since they are also powerful, it is best to stay out of the water when sharks are nearby. Comparatively few fatalities due to shark bite have been reported from Florida and Caribbean waters. However, sharks can cause serious wounds in humans by merely brushing against a swimmer because of their large size and sharp scales.

Considering the many aquatic activities of local people and tourists, it can be said that unprovoked bite attacks on humans by other sea animals also are infrequent. Bites reported to be caused by bluefish and barracuda are probably cases of mistaken identity by the fish. The bluefish are voracious feeders, chasing small fish along the beaches and bathers get in their way; the barracuda sees something flashing in murky water and mistakes it for a fish. Moray bites occur when a diver becomes curious or careless, not realizing that a crevice in the coral he pokes around in is occupied and he is an unwelcome intruder: the moray bites in self defense. Any animal when cornered is potentially dangerous. Do not provoke large marine animals!

Barracuda, great barracuda *(Sphyraena barracuda)*

Miami Seaquarium Photo

LOCATION: Inshore waters and reefs.

HARM TO MAN: Bite wound. Pain and bleeding depending on severity of injury.

PREVENTION: While diving, do not disturb large resting barracudas. Do not wear shiny, flashing objects while diving or snorkeling. Do not trail hands or feet from boat.

AID TO VICTIM: Clean and disinfect wound (see page 56). Get medical attention for large bites, antibiotics if necessary.

REMARKS: Most barracuda bites can be avoided by exercising care. A fisherman bitten in the hand was rinsing off a dolphin fillet in the ocean.

Bluefish *(Pomatomus saltatrix)*

Miami Seaquarium Photo

LOCATION: Seasonal along beaches.

HARM TO MAN: Bite produces puncture wounds, lacerations. Pain and bleeding depends on severity of injury.

PREVENTION: Leave the ocean when feeding schools of bluefish are moving along the beaches. Do not trail hands or feet from boat.

AID TO VICTIM: Clean and disinfect wound (see page 56). Get medical attention, antibiotics if needed.

REMARKS: Along most beaches, lifeguards warn bathers of approaching bluefish schools.

Crocodile, saltwater crocodile *(Crocodylus acutus)*

LOCATION: Shallow shorelines, along banks and mangrove areas.

HARM TO MAN: No reports of crocodile attacks in this area are known. The animals are shy and not seen near populated areas. In other parts of the world, crocodiles are known to attack humans if hungry.

PREVENTION: Do not approach too closely.

REMARKS: The saltwater crocodile is an endangered species in the United States. Known nesting sites exist in only a very few locations in extreme southern Florida. Most of these are in Everglades National Park and closely guarded by rangers. Do not disturb. The American alligator, *Alligator mississippiensis*, has

Photo by Louis Perrero

been implicated in attacks on humans. Alligators are more common than the crocodile in the southeastern United States. They occur farther north to Georgia and Louisiana and prefer freshwater habitats.

Moray, spotted moray (eel) *(Gymnothorax moringa)*

Miami Seaquarium Photo

LOCATION: Reefs and rocky bottom.

9

HARM TO MAN: Bite causes puncture wound. Pain and bleeding.

PREVENTION: Do not provoke eels. Do not put hands into coral crevices. Wear gloves for diving and snorkeling.

AID TO VICTIM: Clean and disinfect wound (see page 56). Attention: mucus may cause infection of wound. Antibiotics if necessary.

REMARKS: Morays do not generally attack people. Another common, possibly dangerous species is the green moray.

Octopus *(Octopus joubini)*

Miami Seaquarium Photo.

LOCATION: Rocky bottom, grassy areas.

HARM TO MAN: Bite produces small circular wound, welt; swelling, pain, nausea, headache, fever, loss of appetite may occur.

PREVENTION: Avoid handling an octopus.

AID TO VICTIM: Remove foreign material. Clean and disinfect wound (see page 56), rest.

REMARKS: Reports of octopus bites are rare. *Octopus vulgaris* is also a potentially dangerous species.

Shark, hammerhead shark *(Sphyrna zygaena)*

Miami Seaquarium Photo

LOCATION: Inshore waters.

HARM TO MAN: Attack may produce bite wound or lacerations, accompanied by pain, loss of blood; injury can be serious, even fatal.

PREVENTION: Leave water when sharks are in the vicinity, avoid splashing, do not carry speared fish on your person.

AID TO VICTIM: Get medical attention. Antibiotics if necessary. Large wounds: attempt to control bleeding with pressure bandages until medical attention is available.

REMARKS: Comparatively few shark attacks occur in Florida and adjacent waters. A number of people are bitten by usually sluggish nurse sharks after grabbing the tail or body of the fish. Other possibly dangerous sharks in these waters:

Blacktip shark	Sand tiger shark
Blue shark	Tiger shark
Lemon shark	White shark
Mako shark	

In fact, any large shark should be considered dangerous.

Toadfish, oyster toadfish *(Opsanus tau)*

LOCATION: Rocky bottom, rubble.

HARM TO MAN: Bite may happen while wading or when fisherman attempts to remove fish from hook. Pain and bleeding.

PREVENTION: Avoid touching fish, wear gloves or use fishing pliers. Wear shoes while wading in shallow water.

AID TO VICTIM: Clean and disinfect wound (see page 56).

Miami Seaquarium Photo

REMARKS: Toadfish are shallow water fish, often lying under rocks, and are easily caught by fishermen. Be careful when removing hook.

Chapter 2.
Animals That Sting

Everyone is familiar with stings by insects that cause great discomfort and, in extreme cases, can result in serious illness and even death. Some marine animals also sting, using structures that vary in size from tiny stinging cells in jellyfish to large spines on sea urchins, fish and rays. Toxic substances are discharged into the wound made by the spines or stinging cells. Of the many venomous animals in the sea only a few are harmful to man. However, serious injury and even death has resulted from their stings. The Portuguese man-of-war *(Physalia)* is virulent. At times the floating jellyfish become abundant and a problem to bathers when onshore winds and currents carry them into shallow water and onto the beaches. Their long tentacles are often not seen by bathers in the water or on the beach where they can be covered with sand or seaweed. Popular swimming beaches are usually closed at these times.

Most people come in contact with a stinging sea animal accidentally, either because they do not know it stings or because they do not see it. In the first category belong the fire coral and fire sponge. They are brightly colored and often serve as hiding places for fish. On a number of local reefs fire coral is one of the predominant structures, yet many people are not aware of this. As another example, cone shells are searched out by shell collectors, yet often amateurs do not know that the animal in the pretty shell can sting. In the second category, sea urchins and rays are often not noticed until the bather or wader steps on one.

Catfish, gafftopsail catfish *(Bagre marinus)*

Miami Seaquarium Photo

LOCATION: Inshore areas.

HARM TO MAN: Stings with pectoral or dorsal fin spines; causes painful puncture wound, swelling.

PREVENTION: Avoid spines on fins when handling.

AID TO VICTIM: Remove foreign material. Clean and disinfect wound (see page 56).

REMARKS: Fishermen may encounter these fish when angling or net fishing and be injured by the sharp spines when removing them from a hook or a net.

Catfish, sea catfish *(Arius felis)*

LOCATION: Inshore areas.

HARM TO MAN: Stings by spiny rays on fins cause painful puncture wounds, swelling.

PREVENTION: Avoid spines on fins.

AID TO VICTIM: Remove foreign material. Clean and disinfect wound (see page 56).

Miami Seaquarium Photo

REMARKS: This is a frequently caught catfish, but is not popular as a food fish. It is considered a nuisance by anglers who find it difficult to take these catfish off the hook without being hurt by their sharp spines.

Cone shell *(Conus spurius* plus several subspecies and *C. ermineus)*

LOCATION: Rubble bottom *(C. ermineus)* and sandy bottom *(C. spurius).*

HARM TO MAN: Contact with venomous stinging apparatus of cone shell produces puncture wound associated with immediate, sometimes intense pain on

14

site of injury, later numbness. Tingling of mouth area and extremities may develop, also tremor, nausea, vomiting, dizziness and respiratory distress.

PREVENTION: Shell collectors should use gloves. Be careful when handling cone shells. Do not carry them close to body.

AID TO VICTIM: Remove foreign material from wound. Soak in hot water. In severe case get medical attention.

REMARKS: Venom apparatus of cone shells dangerous to man is generally used by cone to capture small fish. Not all cones are equally venomous. No record exists of poisoning from Florida or the Caribbean, but in other parts of the world fatalities or serious cases have been reported. Caution in handling cones is advised especially if they are known to be capable of paralyzing or killing fish, such as *Conus ermineus*.

Coral, fire coral *(Millepora* spp.)

Photo by Jim LaTourrette, Miami Seaquarium

LOCATION: Reefs and bridge pilings.

HARM TO MAN: Contact with fire coral produces welts, itching, pain, skin irritation.

PREVENTION: Wear gloves while diving on reefs. Avoid contact with fire coral.

AID TO VICTIM: Apply alcohol or other antiseptic solution.

REMARKS: Fire coral is very common on many Florida reefs. It can best be recognized by its orange-yellow color and the arrangement of tiny pores in groups of six, a central larger one surrounded by five smaller ones.

Jellyfish, moon jellyfish *(Aurelia aurita)*

LOCATION: Drifting in open sea and near shore.

HARM TO MAN: Contact produces itching, pain, localized redness and welts, skin irritation.

PREVENTION: Avoid contact.

AID TO VICTIM: Apply alcohol or solution of ammonia. Other remedies: vinegar, lemon juice, soap.

REMARKS: The moon jellyfish can appear in large numbers. They grow to a size of about 1 ft. (30 cm.) in diameter.

Man-of-war; Portuguese man-of-war *(Physalia physalis)*

LOCATION: Open water and beaches.

HARM TO MAN: Contact with tentacles which contain venomous stinging apparatus causes red welts on skin, itching, pain, possibly fever, vomiting, paralysis. Tentacles may cling to victim. Breathing may become difficult, the pulse rate rapid and feeble. May cause unconsciousness.

PREVENTION: Stay out of ocean when warning signs are posted on beaches. Stay a safe distance away from man-of-war's gas float when swimming. Do not disturb man-of-war on beaches as the tentacles may spatter if the gas float bursts.

AID TO VICTIM: Remove all clinging tentacles from victim's body with towel or clothing. Apply alcohol or sun lotion to stop further action of nematocysts (stinging cells). External antihistamine creams and oral antihistamines help. Other external

Miami Seaquarium Photo

remedies: sugar, soap, vinegar, lemon juice, ammonia solution, sodium bicarbonate, boric acid solution, papain. Also, apply shaving cream and then shave the affected part with a safety razor. In severe cases, get medical attention.

REMARKS: Usually the biggest invasion of man-of-war in Florida occurs during spring. Warning signs are then posted along the beaches. If a man-of-war washes ashore do not step on the tentacles because they continue to sting for some time even when dry.

Another dangerous warm water stinging jellyfish is the sea wasp, which is rare in this area.

Scorpion fish, barbfish *(Scorpaena brasiliensis)*

Photo by J. Randall

LOCATION: Rocky bottom.

17

HARM TO MAN: Venomous sting by dorsal and possibly anal and pelvic fin spines causes puncture wounds, pain, swelling, sometimes nausea, vomiting, headache, diarrhea.

PREVENTION: Use footwear while wading, avoid contact. Fishermen: be careful when removing hooked scorpion fish.

AID TO VICTIM: Remove foreign material from wound, soak in hot water, disinfect (see page 56). If necessary, get medical attention.

REMARKS: Barbfish lie quietly in shallow water. They are hard to see because of their protective color.

Sea urchin *(Diadema antillarum)*

Photo by J. Randall

LOCATION: Rocky bottom, reefs, grass beds, pilings, sea walls.

HARM TO MAN: Stepping on or accidentally touching sea urchin spines may produce puncture wounds contaminated with sea urchin poison, causing immediate intense pain, localized swelling and redness; in more severe cases nausea and respiratory difficulties. Spines broken off in victim's skin can cause infection.

PREVENTION: Avoid contact. Watch where you step while wading. Use some kind of footwear in shallows or reefs.

AID TO VICTIM: Remove spines and other foreign particles from wound, disinfect (see page 56). In serious cases seek medical attention.

REMARKS: Many sea urchins are not poisonous. However since most have sharp spines it is best to avoid them. Eating gonads (eggs) of sea urchins may cause intoxication.

Sponge, fire or red sponge *(Tedania ignis)*

Photo by Billy B. Boothe, Jr.

LOCATION: Grass flats or hard bottom, mangrove roots.

HARM TO MAN: Touching fire sponge may cause stinging sensation, itching, pain, welts, swelling, skin reaction similar to poison ivy.

PREVENTION: Beware of all red or orange-colored sponges. Avoid contact, wear gloves when diving or snorkeling.

AID TO VICTIM: Soak in dilute acetic acid (commercial vinegar) or use antiseptic dressings.

REMARKS: This non-commercial sponge is easily recognized by its bright red or orange color. Chemical irritants are released upon contact. The spicules apparently do not pierce the skin.

Sting ray, southern sting ray *(Dasyatis americana)*

LOCATION: Grass beds, sandy bottom.

HARM TO MAN: Contact with venomous spine in tail of ray causes both lacerations and poisoning. Intense, rapidly spreading pain. Poisoning symptoms mostly limited to injured area. Possibly weakness, nausea, and anxiety. Less frequently observed are vomiting, diarrhea, sweating, respiratory distress.

PREVENTION: Wear shoes while wading. Shuffle feet on sandy bottom. Do not pick up rays.

Miami Seaquarium Photo

AID TO VICTIM: Remove foreign material. Soak in hot water for 30-90 minutes. Severe lacerations need medical attention, less severe wounds should be disinfected (see page 56).

REMARKS: Sting rays do not attack man. The tail spine is used by the ray as a defensive weapon.

Cowfish, scrawled cowfish *(Lactophrys quadricornis)* and Trunkfish *(Lactophrys trigonus)*

Miami Seaquarium Photo

LOCATION: Reefs, inshore areas.

HARM TO MAN: Handling these fish may cause puncture wounds; pain, bleeding, swelling.

20

PREVENTION: Wear gloves when handling.

AID TO VICTIM: Clean and disinfect wound (see page 56).

REMARKS: Anglers and net fishermen should handle these fish with care.

Worm, bristle worm *(Hermodice carunculata)*

Photo by J. Randall

LOCATION: Reefs, inshore rubble.

HARM TO MAN: Contact with worm's bristles causes burning sensation, swelling, numbness, skin irritation.

PREVENTION: Avoid contact.

AID TO VICTIM: Remove bristles stuck in victim's skin with tweezers, apply ammonia or alcohol.

REMARKS: Usually found under rocks, this worm should not be handled without gloves.

Chapter 3.
Animals That Are Dangerous to Eat

POISONOUS ANIMALS

Types of poisoning associated with eating fish are ciguatera, scombroid, and puffer poisoning. These poisons should not be confused with ptomaine poisons produced in a variety of foods by spoilage.

Ciguatera is apparently caused by fish feeding on toxic algae and accumulating the poison in their flesh. When these fish are eaten by other fish the poison becomes more concentrated. Ciguatera usually occurs in reef or shore fish. It is quite possible that fish from one area of a reef are poisonous, but not from another nearby area. About 300 species of fish have been implicated in this type of poisoning. Most of them are normally edible. Since there are no outward signs or symptoms by which to distinguish poisonous from non-poisonous individuals this form of fish-poisoning is treacherous.

Scombroid poisoning found in mackerels and tunas is different from ciguatera in that it is caused by bacterial action in the fish's muscle tissue after death which produces a poisonous substance called scombrotoxin. It can be avoided by putting the catch on ice immediately.

Puffers manufacture their own poison. It occurs in the liver, intestines, skin, and reproductive organs. Since it is a very strong poison known to cause fatalities, puffers should not be eaten.

For more detail on symptoms caused by these poisons, see page 56.

Amberjack, greater amberjack *(Seriola dumerili)*

Miami Seaquarium Photo

LOCATION: Open ocean.

HARM TO MAN: Ciguatera poisoning.

SYMPTOMS: Can be severe. Weakness, abdominal pain, vomiting, diarrhea, headache, dizziness, tingling and numbness of the lips, tongue and throat, skin rash, convulsions, often reversal of feeling of hot and cold may occur.

PREVENTION: Do not eat large amberjack. The toxin is not destroyed by cooking.

AID TO VICTIM: No known antidote, treatment is symptomatic. Medical treatment is directed toward eliminating poison from body.

REMARKS: It is recommended not to eat amberjack in the Leeward Islands of the West Indies.

Barracuda, great barracuda *(Sphyraena barracuda)*

Miami Seaquarium Photo

LOCATION: Inshore areas, reefs.

HARM TO MAN: Ciguatera poisoning.

SYMPTOMS: Can be severe. Weakness, abdominal pain, vomiting, diarrhea, headache, dizziness, tingling and numbness of the lips, tongue and throat, skin rash, convulsions, often reversal of feeling of hot and cold may occur.

PREVENTION: Do not eat large barracuda over 2 lbs. (900 gms). Do not eat fish from areas where ciguatera was recently reported. Seek local knowledge.

AID TO VICTIM: No known antidote. Treatment is symptomatic. Medical treatment is directed toward eliminating poison from body.

Conch, queen or pink conch *(Strombus gigas)*

LOCATION: Sandy areas, grass beds, rubble bottom.

HARM TO MAN: Presence of ciguatera-like poison in flesh of conch may cause "ciguatera" poisoning in man.

SYMPTOMS: Nausea, vomiting, abdominal pain, weakness, diarrhea.

PREVENTION: Avoid eating conchs with very heavy or eroded shells. Avoid eating conch from an area where ciguatera is present. Seek local knowledge.

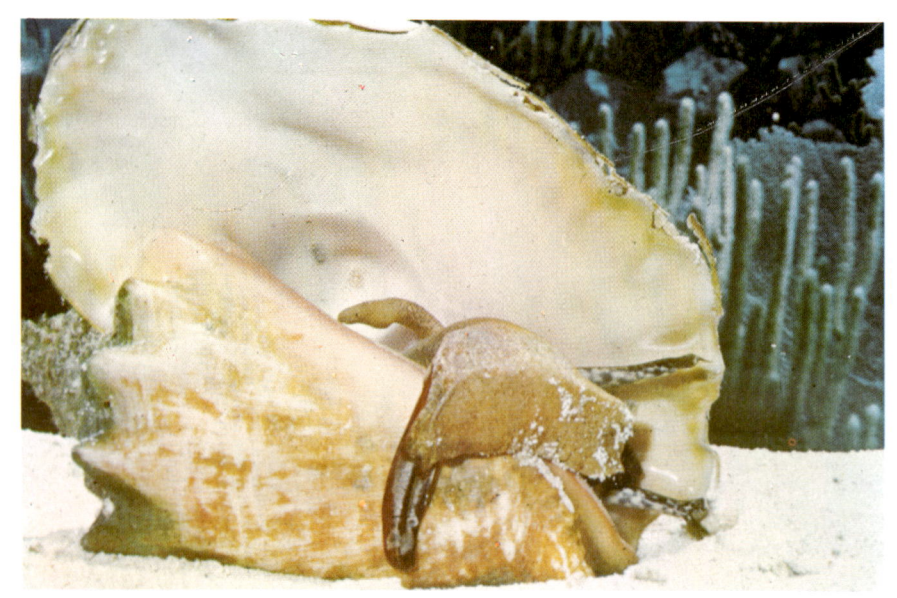

Miami Seaquarium Photo

AID TO VICTIM: No known antidote. Treatment is symptomatic. Medical attention indicated.

Filefish, fringed filefish *(Monacanthus ciliatus)*

Miami Seaquarium Photo

24

LOCATION: Reefs.

HARM TO MAN: Ciguatera poisoning.

SYMPTOMS: Can be severe. Weakness, abdominal pain, vomiting, diarrhea, headache, dizziness, tingling and numbness of the lips, tongue and throat, skin rash, convulsions, often reversal of feeling of hot and cold may occur.

PREVENTION: Do not eat fish from areas where ciguatera is reported. Seek local knowledge.

AID TO VICTIM: No known antidote. Treatment is symptomatic. Medical treatment is directed toward eliminating poison from body.

Goatfish, yellow goatfish *(Mulloidichthys martinicus)* and Spotted goatfish *(Pseudupeneus maculatus)*

Miami Seaquarium Photo

LOCATION: Reefs, grass beds.

HARM TO MAN: Ciguatera poisoning.

SYMPTOMS: Can be severe. Weakness, abdominal pain, vomiting, diarrhea, headache, dizziness, tingling and numbness of the lips, tongue and throat, skin rash, convulsions, often reversal of feeling of hot and cold may occur.

PREVENTION: Do not eat fish from areas where ciguatera is reported. Seek local knowledge.

AID TO VICTIM: No known antidote. Treatment is symptomatic. Medical treatment is directed toward eliminating poison from body.

Hogfish *(Lachnolaimus maximus)*

Miami Seaquarium Photo

LOCATION: Reefs.

HARM TO MAN: Ciguatera poisoning.

SYMPTOMS: Can be severe. Weakness, abdominal pain, vomiting, diarrhea, headache, dizziness, tingling and numbness of the lips, tongue and throat, skin rash, convulsions, often reversal of feeling of hot and cold may occur.

PREVENTION: Do not eat fish from areas where ciguatera is reported. Seek local knowledge.

AID TO VICTIM: No known antidote. Treatment is symptomatic. Medical treatment is directed toward eliminating poison from body.

Jack, crevalle jack *(Caranx hippos)*

LOCATION: Inshore waters, reefs.

HARM TO MAN: Ciguatera poisoning.

SYMPTOMS: Can be severe. Weakness, abdominal pain, vomiting, diarrhea, headache, dizziness, tingling and numbness of the lips, tongue and throat, skin rash, convulsions, often reversal of feeling of hot and cold may occur.

PREVENTION: Do not eat large jacks. Do not eat fish from areas where ciguatera is reported. Seek local knowledge.

Photo by F. Berry, NMFS

AID TO VICTIM: No known antidote. Treatment is symptomatic. Medical treatment is directed toward eliminating poison from the body.

REMARKS: Many jacks have been reported to cause ciguatera poisoning, especially in the northeast Caribbean.

Mackerel, king mackerel (kingfish) *(Scomberomorus cavalla)*

Photo by F. Berry, NMFS

LOCATION: Open ocean.

HARM TO MAN: Scombroid poisoning.

SYMPTOMS: Redness of the skin, face flushed and swollen, headache, dizziness, circulatory problems, stomach distress.

PREVENTION: Fish should be put on ice as soon as caught. Do not leave your catch in the sun, do not eat fish if it has a "peppery" taste.

AID TO VICTIM: Antihistamine drugs and other clinical methods.

REMARKS: Mainly reported from the Caribbean. Also reported from wahoo, Spanish mackerel, and cero mackerel, and possibly other fish.

Moray, green moray *(Gymnothorax funebris)*

Miami Seaquarium Photo

LOCATION: Reefs, rocky bottom.

HARM TO MAN: Ciguatera-like poisoning.

SYMPTOMS: Can be severe. Weakness, abdominal pain, vomiting, diarrhea, headache, dizziness, tingling and numbness of the lips, tongue and throat, skin rash, convulsions, often reversal of feeling of hot and cold may occur.

PREVENTION: Do not eat morays.

AID TO VICTIM: No known antidote. Treatment is symptomatic.

REMARKS: Other moray species are also implicated in this type of poisoning.

Parrotfish, blue parrotfish *(Scarus coeruleus)*

LOCATION: Reefs and inshore waters.

HARM TO MAN: Ciguatera poisoning.

SYMPTOMS: Can be severe. Weakness, abdominal pain, vomiting, diarrhea, headache, dizziness, tingling and numbness of the lips, tongue and throat, skin rash, convulsions, often reversal of feeling of hot and cold may occur.

PREVENTION: Do not eat fish from areas where ciguatera is reported. Seek local knowledge.

Miami Seaquarium Photo

AID TO VICTIM: No known antidote. Treatment is symptomatic. Medical treatment is directed toward eliminating poison from body.

REMARKS: Other parrotfish species are also implicated in causing this type of poisoning.

Porcupinefish *(Diodon hystrix)*

Miami Seaquarium Photo

LOCATION: Inshore waters, reefs.

HARM TO MAN: Puffer poisoning.

SYMPTOMS: Lethargy, muscular weakness, dizziness, nausea, numbness, respiratory distress, possibly paralysis in severe cases and death.

PREVENTION: Do not eat porcupinefish.

AID TO VICTIM: No known antidote. Treatment is symptomatic. Get medical attention.

REMARKS: Despite the health hazard, some people still eat porcupinefish. This is dangerous because during cleaning the intestines, liver, skin and reproductive organs which are the sources of the poison may contaminate the flesh. Very poisonous.

Puffer, checkered puffer *(Sphoeroides testudineus)*

Miami Seaquarium Photo

LOCATION: Rocky bottom, inshore waters.

HARM TO MAN: Puffer poisoning.

SYMPTOMS: Lethargy, muscular weakness, dizziness, nausea, numbness, respiratory distress, paralysis. Death in severe cases due to respiratory paralysis.

PREVENTION: Do not eat puffers.

AID TO VICTIM: No known antidote, treatment is symptomatic. Get medical attention.

REMARKS: Despite the health hazard, some people still eat puffers. This is dangerous because during cleaning the intestines, liver, skin and reproductive organs which are the sources of the poison may contaminate the flesh. Very poisonous; fatalities known in Asia from a related species.

Sharks, great white shark *(Carcharodon carcharias)*
Hammerhead *(Sphyrna zygaena)*

great white shark

hammerhead shark

LOCATION: Inshore and open ocean.

HARM TO MAN: Elasmobranch poisoning, thought to be a form of ciguatera poisoning.

SYMPTOMS: Nausea, vomiting, abdominal pain, diarrhea, headache, possibly respiratory distress.

PREVENTION: Do not eat large sharks or fish from areas where poisoning is reported. Do not eat shark livers.

AID TO VICTIM: No known antidote. Treatment is symptomatic. Get medical attention if necessary.

REMARKS: Poison is often concentrated in the liver. Although fatalities are known to occur, none have been reported from Florida and vicinity.

Snapper, mangrove or grey snapper *(Lutjanus griseus)*

Miami Seaquarium Photo

LOCATION: Inshore waters, reefs.

HARM TO MAN: Ciguatera poisoning.

SYMPTOMS: Can be severe. Weakness, abdominal pain, vomiting, diarrhea, headache, dizziness, tingling and numbness of the lips, tongue and throat, skin rash, convulsions, often reversal of feeling of hot and cold may occur.

PREVENTION: Do not eat snapper from areas where ciguatera is reported. Seek local knowledge.

AID TO VICTIM: No known antidote. Treatment is symptomatic. Clinical treatment is directed toward eliminating poison from body.

Surgeonfish, ocean surgeon *(Acanthurus bahianus)*

LOCATION: Reefs.

HARM TO MAN: Ciguatera poisoning.

SYMPTOMS: Can be severe. Weakness, abdominal pain, vomiting, diarrhea, headache, dizziness, tingling and numbness of the lips, tongue and throat, skin rash, convulsions, often reversal of feeling of hot and cold may occur.

PREVENTION: Do not eat fish from areas where ciguatera is reported. Seek local knowledge.

Miami Seaquarium Photo

AID TO VICTIM: No known antidote. Treatment is symptomatic. Clinical treatment is directed toward eliminating poison from body.

Triggerfish, ocean triggerfish *(Canthidermis sufflamen)*

Miami Seaquarium Photo

LOCATION: Open water, reefs.

HARM TO MAN: Ciguatera poisoning.

SYMPTOMS: Can be severe. Weakness, abdominal pain, vomiting, diarrhea, headache, dizziness, tingling and numbness of the lips, tongue and throat, skin rash, convulsions, often reversal of feeling of hot and cold may occur.

PREVENTION: Do not eat fish from areas where ciguatera is reported. Seek local knowledge.

AID TO VICTIM: No known antidote. Treatment is symptomatic. Medical treatment is directed toward eliminating poison from body.

REMARKS: Queen triggerfish, *Balistes vetula,* is suspected of being poisonous in the Caribbean.

Trunkfish *(Lactophrys trigonus)*

Miami Seaquarium Photo

LOCATION: Inshore areas.

HARM TO MAN: Puffer-like poisoning, possibly toxic liver. Also, may cause ciguatera.

SYMPTOMS: Similar to puffer poisoning: Weakness, numbness, dizziness, nausea, respiratory distress.

PREVENTION: Do not eat trunkfish.

AID TO VICTIM: No known antidote. Treatment is symptomatic. Seek medical attention.

Tuna, skipjack tuna *(Euthynnus pelamis)*

LOCATION: Open ocean.

HARM TO MAN: Scombroid poisoning.

SYMPTOMS: Redness of the skin, face flushed and swollen, headache, dizziness, circulatory problems, stomach distress.

PREVENTION: Fish should be put on ice as soon as caught. Do not leave your catch lying in the sun, do not eat fish if it has a "peppery" taste.

Photo by F. Berry, NMFS

AID TO VICTIM: Antihistamine drugs and other clinical methods.

REMARKS: Mainly reported from the Caribbean. In addition to skipjack this poison has been reported from mackerels, wahoo, and possibly other fish.

Turtle, hawksbill turtle *(Eretmochelys imbricata)*

Miami Seaquarium Photo

LOCATION: Open ocean and beaches.

HARM TO MAN: Ciguatera-like poisoning. Possibly caused by the turtle's diet, toxic algae. The toxin is retained in the flesh.

SYMPTOMS: Vomiting, limb pains, skin rash; in severe cases coma and death.

PREVENTION: Do not eat turtles from areas where ciguatera is present. Seek local knowledge.

AID TO VICTIM: No known antidote. Treatment is symptomatic. Get medical attention.

REMARKS: Apparently no cases reported from this area, only Asia.

ANIMALS CONTAINING POLLUTANTS

Due to the effects of man's pollution of natural waters, marine animals may become diseased or die. This is of considerable concern to environmentalists, but of even greater immediate concern is the possible effect on humans by eating fish and shellfish from polluted waters.

Untreated or insufficiently treated sewage is one source of pollution. Some shellfish and mollusks take in viruses and bacteria, and tend to accumulate the poisons produced by them. These microorganisms and their wastes can cause diseases in humans, including hepatitis (inflammation of the liver), typhoid fever (bacteria causing cramps and diarrhea), and paralytic shellfish poisoning. The latter disease has caused deaths in 10-25 percent of cases reported. One group of bacteria, *Vibrio,* found in shellfish causes intestinal disorders in humans.

Among the many kinds of waste that man releases into the sea are pesticides, heavy metals, hydrocarbons, and chlorinated hydrocarbons. Finfish and shellfish can accumulate these pollutants and will then be harmful to man if eaten.

The most publicized and serious case of heavy metal poisoning occurred in Japan from 1953-1961. There, mercury released from industrial processes was accumulated in the tissues of fish and shellfish, and caused the death of 46 persons and 100 others suffered serious neurological disturbances from chronic poisoning in the year 1953 alone.

Although many other pollutants accumulate in fish and shellfish, at this time, the evidence of them being human health hazards is not as strong as it is for mercury. Nonetheless, it is strongly recommended to avoid eating fish or shellfish from areas contaminated with industrial or domestic pollutants.

Even in relatively unpolluted areas, shellfish can acquire poisons harmful to humans. Tiny drifting single-celled organisms in the sea at times become very abundant, or "bloom." They serve as food for shellfish and release poisons that are accumulated in the tissues.

Some fish and shellfish may become diseased by pollutants present in the water. These toxic substances may act as irritants on the fish and produce or contribute to *clearly visible* sores (lesions), protrusions of eye balls (exophthalmia) and fin rot. These diseased animals are unsightly and unappetizing. Furthermore, since they have been in contact with toxins, they may have accumulated pollutants in the flesh that would make them poisonous for humans to eat.

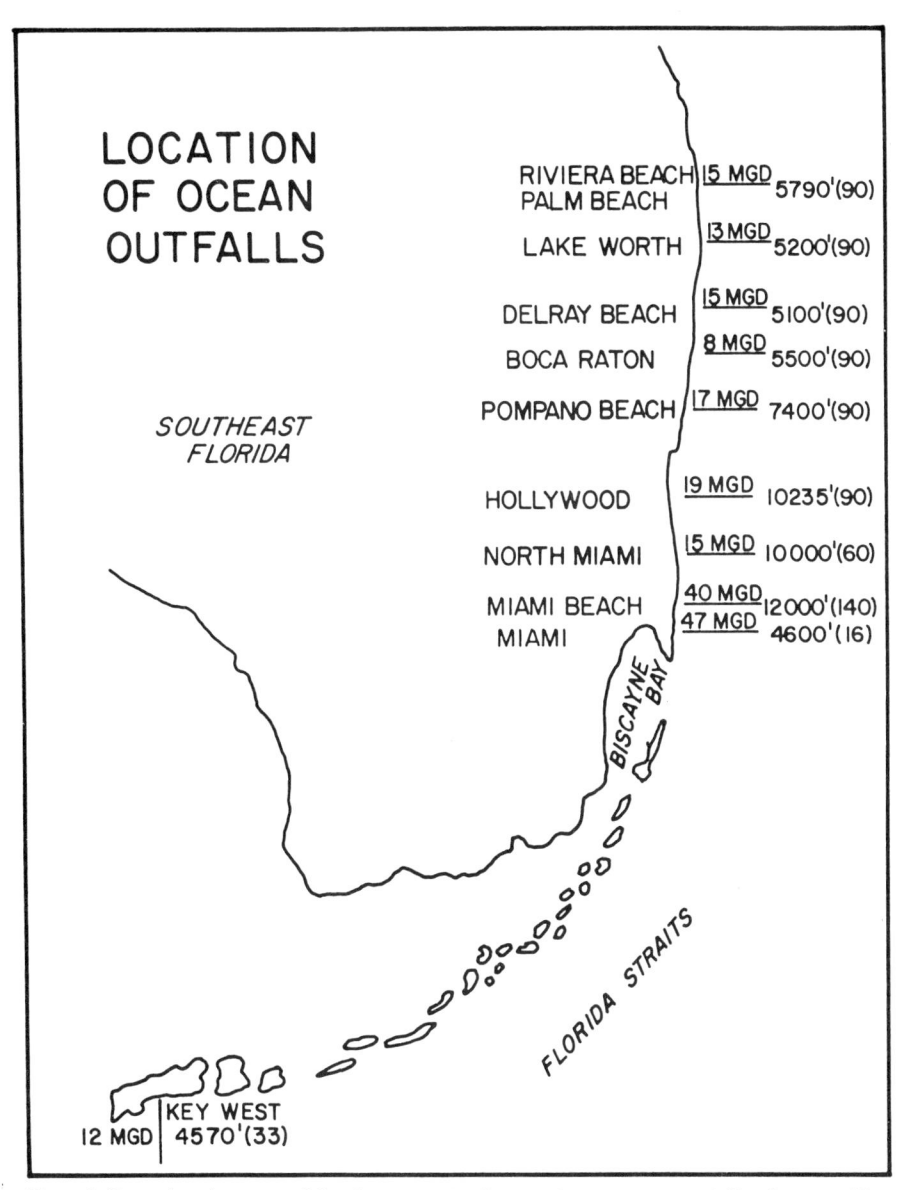

Figure 1. Examples of ocean outfalls releasing variously treated sewage into south Florida waters. The MGD number = million gallons/day, the next number = length of the pipe from shore (in feet) and the number in parenthesis = depth (in feet) at the point of discharge. (From Lee and McGuire, 1973, University of Miami Sea Grant Program, Bulletin Number 2)

Oyster, *(Crassostrea virginica)*

LOCATION: Mangrove roots, flats, inshore banks.

HARM TO MAN: Gastrointestinal disturbance, hepatitis.

37

CAUSE: Bacterial contamination caused by sewage or other man-made pollution in water surrounding oyster beds.

SYMPTOMS: Upset stomach, diarrhea, vomiting.

PREVENTION: Only eat oysters from non-polluted waters.

AID TO VICTIM: Get medical attention in severe cases.

REMARKS: Public health authorities can provide information on safety of local oyster beds.

Oyster, *(Crassostrea virginica* and *C. rhizophorae)*

LOCATION: Mangroves, flats, inshore banks.

HARM TO MAN: Paralytic shellfish poisoning.

CAUSE: Biotoxins accumulated by oysters.

SYMPTOMS: Tingling of lips, tongue, face, which may turn to numbness, constrictive sensation in throat, incoherent speech. Dizziness, headache, weakness, perspiration; respiratory distress and paralysis may occur.

PREVENTION: Avoid eating shellfish from areas where known cases are being reported. Obtain this information from local health authorities.

AID TO VICTIM: No specific antidote. Treatment is largely symptomatic. Medical attention indicated.

State of Maryland, Department of Economic and Community Development

REMARKS: Public health authorities give out information on safety of local oyster beds.

Reef fish such as snappers, groupers, grunts, jacks, etc.

Miami Seaquarium Photo

LOCATION: Inshore.

HARM TO MAN: Possible health disturbances when eating fish containing pollutants.

39

CAUSE: Contamination of fish by pollution.

SYMPTOMS: Undetermined.

PREVENTION: Do not eat fish caught near sources of domestic, industrial or agricultural pollution.

REMARKS: The amount of pollutants that humans can ingest from fish tissues without ill effects has not been determined.

DISEASED AND PARASITIZED ANIMALS

Sometimes a freshly-caught fish will have an unappetizing appearance due to the presence of parasites, although it has no other unpleasant characteristics. Is such a fish safe to eat?

The salt water angler has reason to be concerned about parasites in his fish. The appearance of the flesh and even flavor may be marred, or in some cases the person eating the fish may become infected with the parasite.

From the tiniest one-celled animals to the giant whales, every animal species plays host to parasites of one kind or another (Fig. 2). In some animals parasites of different kinds can be found inhabiting almost every organ or surface area. Some are even small enough to live within the animal's cells. The Pacific sockeye salmon is host to more than fifty different parasites.

Fortunately for the fish (and for the fisherman's peace of mind), many parasites that attach to the outside of reef fish and other inshore fish are removed and eaten by smaller fish and shrimp. These parasite-cleaning creatures provide a most interesting example of cooperation between animals of different species. They remove parasites from the skin, gills, fins and mouths of other animals.

The angler may not see many of the parasites in his catch because they are often located in such parts as entrails and gills, which are discarded. Since very heavily infected fish become weakened and may fall prey to larger fish, birds, or mammals, they are not often caught by anglers.

The parasites that fishermen are most likely to find are on the skin (ectoparasites) or in the flesh (endoparasites). "Anchor worms" *(Pennella)* (not worms at all, but copepods, relatives of barnacles and lobsters) are easily seen. These creatures bury their heads in the flesh of the host fish and leave their bodies protruding. Other close relatives of copepods called "fish lice" *(Argulus)* also occur on the skin of fishes. Occasionally, leeches, or "blood suckers," sea-going relatives of the earthworm, attach to the skin of fishes and are found by fishermen. They are attached so loosely that they sometimes let go of the host when it is caught. Because anchor worms, fish lice, and blood suckers can easily be removed by the angler when the fish is skinned or scaled, they present little problem.

Parasites located in the flesh of food-fishes are of greater concern to the angler. These are generally of three kinds: protozoans (single-celled animals), roundworms, and flatworms.

Protozoans occur as small cysts scattered through the body muscles of fish. These cysts, resembling tapioca, are spherical and contain numerous protozoans.

There is no intermediate host involved in the transmission of this parasite. For the protozoan to infect another fish it must be eaten by another fish, either of the same or a related species. Spanish mackerel harbor a species of protozoan in the flesh, but in this case, as in many others, the parasite is harmless to man.

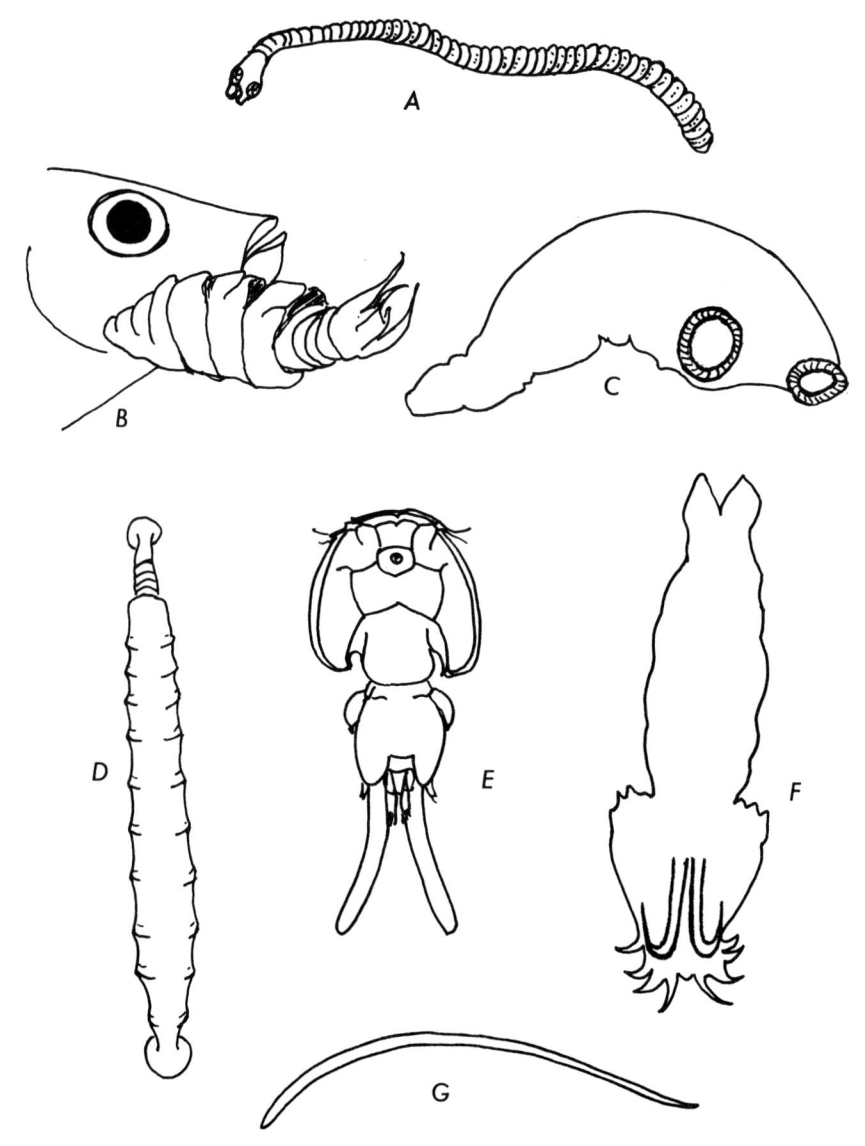

Figure 2. Examples of the larger, more common adult parasites of marine fish and shellfish. (A) tapeworm (flatworm), found in fish gut, (B) isopod, on gills, mouth or head, (C) digenetic trematode (flatworm), in fish gut, (D) leech, on outside of fish, (E) copepod (crustacean) on outside of fish or on gills, (F) monogenetic trematode (flatworm) on gills or outside of fish, (G) nematode (roundworm) in fish gut. These parasites usually range in size from about 0.25 to 2.5 cm (1/16 to 1 inch).

Roundworms may also be found encysted in the flesh of some southern marine fishes, such as the red drum and the wahoo. Usually only a few roundworms occur in each fish, but many members of any particular species of fish may be infected. When these infected fish are eaten by birds, or by mammals such as seals or porpoises, the young worms grow to adults and reproduce. The life cycle cannot be completed unless this final host eats an infected fish. Recent reports of accidental infection of humans are known from South America, Asia, and Polynesian islands.

In the body muscles of some fish, anglers may notice "grubs." These are the young (larval) stages of flatworms. The life cycles of some of these flatworm parasites are extremely complicated (Fig. 3). Each species has a number of stages during which it must live in certain organs of two or more host species in order to complete the life cycle. For example, the young stages may occur in certain snails (or shellfish), and the adult stages may occur in fish. In seatrout, the angler may find these grubs entwined in the muscles. At certain times of the year, usually during summer, half of the seatrout catch may be infected. Some of the larger trout may have more than 100 of these worms, some of which may be over 6 in. (15 cm) long. The possibility of accidental human infection, although never reported from this area, warrants the recommendation not to eat raw fish dishes.

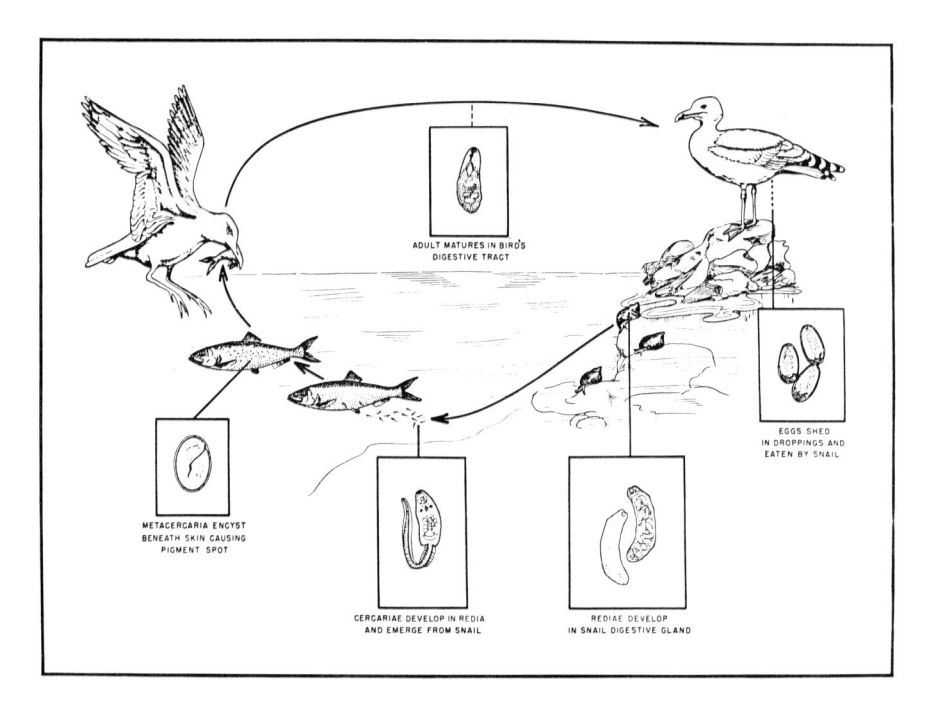

Figure 3. A typical life cycle of a flatworm parasite in fish involving several hosts (snail, fish, bird). (From Sindermann and Farrin, 1962, Ecology Vol. 43).

What guidelines can the angler use to decide on whether or not to eat his fish?

Generally, if a parasite is so abundant in a fish that it is difficult to remove from the flesh, a disagreeable flavor will result. In any case, the flesh will not be very appetizing. However, effects on flavor and appearance may be very important to one person while not to another; it is a matter of individual taste. The important consideration is the possible danger of infection to man.

There is a widely-held notion that open-water fish are safe to eat raw. Raw skipjack tuna is an important item in the diets of many Asians. In Hawaii, some tunas and a species of mackerel are popular in raw form. Fresh fish are cut into thin slices which are dipped into soy sauce mixed with grated ginger or mustard. People not accustomed to the strong sauce often argue that it would kill any worm on contact, but that is merely conjecture. In another popular raw-fish dish called lomilomi (Hawaiian for "massage"), the fish flesh is mashed with the fingers, and relish, onions or peppers are added to taste. Based on past records, the notion that open-water fish are safe to eat raw seems to be true. Some species of fresh-water fish parasites are known to infect man, but the vast majority of parasites of open ocean fish have never been known to do this. Perhaps this is because fish parasites from the open sea are not adapted to develop into adults using man as a host. Many people besides Asians like raw fish. To be on the safe side it is best to cook fish.

Although cooking kills most of the parasites, it does not guarantee destruction of all encysted worms. A series of experiments sponsored by the U.S. Public Health Service showed that the hot-smoking procedure in which fish are smoked from two to four hours at temperatures of 110° to 250°F (43° to 121°C) will apparently kill all encysted worms. Unfortunately, most smoked fish is prepared by a cold-smoking method and no data were collected on the effect of this process on encysted worms. In this method, cooler temperatures, generally under 100°F (38°C) and usually about 75°F (24°C) are used, and the fish are hung a considerable distance from the fire. The smoke cools before it reaches the fish and although the fish fillets are exposed to the smoke for an extended time, the temperatures in the flesh where the worms are encysted may be too low to kill them. Even stronger preservation methods may not harm these worms. In the same series of experiments, larval worms in fish frozen for five days died but those in a strong brine solution remained alive for a month.

Thoroughly cooking any fish, whether caught in fresh water, brackish water or salt water, will eliminate all danger from parasites. But to be doubly safe, it is wise to cut from the flesh any worms or other obviously foreign organisms. If you miss some, however, the chances are that you will never know the difference and they will not bother you.

NON-PARASITIC DISEASES OF FISH AND SHELLFISH

Fish may become sick and die because of human pollution. However, there are many diseases of fish and shellfish that result from natural causes in addition to parasites and quite apart from man's domestic, industrial and agricultural pollution. These natural causes such as acute temperature changes, decomposition of organic matter, lack of oxygen and poisons released by tiny floating organisms (i.e., red tide caused by plankton) are hard to pinpoint. Fish diseased or distressed from these natural causes usually occur in large numbers and are accompanied by dead or dying fish. Furthermore, these diseases affect not only many fish, but fish of many different species.

Since the cause of disease is generally not known or difficult to determine, it is advisable not to eat fish that are behaving unnaturally, or are caught in the vicinity of dead or dying fish.

Bluefish *(Pomatomus saltatrix)*

Miami Seaquarium Photo

LOCATION: Open ocean, seasonally on beaches.

DISEASE OR CONDITION: Isopod infestation.

GROSS SIGNS: Isopod in mouth or gill cavity.

EFFECT ON MAN: None.

REMARKS: This ectoparasite can easily be removed during cleaning of fish.

Blue crab *(Callinectes sapidus)*

LOCATION: Inshore areas.

DISEASE OR CONDITION: Pepper spots.

GROSS SIGNS: Black pepper-like spots in muscle of crab.

Miami Seaquarium Photo

CAUSE: Parasitic infection by Protozoa (one-celled animals).

EFFECT ON MAN: Unappetizing.

REMARKS: This parasite is destroyed by cooking.

Blue crab *(Callinectes sapidus)*

State of Maryland, Department of Economic and Community Development

LOCATION: Inshore areas.

DISEASE OR CONDITION: Shell disease.

GROSS SIGNS: Discolored, soft, and eroded crab shell.

CAUSE: Possibly bacteria.

EFFECT ON MAN: Unappetizing.

REMARKS: This condition apparently does not affect the quality or flavor of the meat.

45

Drum, black drum *(Pogonias cromis)*
Striped drum, high-hat *(Equetus acuminatus)*

black drum

striped drum   Miami Seaquarium Photo

LOCATION: Inshore waters, rocky bottom.

DISEASE OR CONDITION: Tapeworm infection.

GROSS SIGNS: Long ribbon-like white worm larvae in flesh.

EFFECT ON MAN: Some tapeworm larvae can become parasites of man when ingested with raw fish dishes. Reported from Japan to Peru, so far not from this area.

REMARKS: These worms are more often found in fish in the summer. Remove parasites. Cook fish well. Avoid raw fish dishes (cebiche, sashimi, etc.)

Flounder, peacock flounder *(Bothus lunatus)*

Miami Seaquarium Photo

LOCATION: Sandy bottom.

DISEASE OR CONDITION: Roundworm infection.

GROSS SIGNS: Round-bodied worm larvae in flesh or other organs, either free or encysted.

EFFECT ON MAN: Accidental infection in humans can cause enteritis and meningioencephalitis. No cases reported from this area.

REMARKS: More infected fish are reported during the summer. Clean and cook fish well. Avoid eating raw fish.

Grouper, Nassau grouper *(Epinephelus striatus)*

LOCATION: Rocky bottom, reefs.

DISEASE OR CONDITION: Roundworm infection.

GROSS SIGNS: Round-bodied worm larvae of varying size in flesh or other organs, either free or encysted.

EFFECT ON MAN: Accidentally ingested roundworm larvae can cause enteritis and meningioencephalitis. No reported cases from this area.

Miami Seaquarium Photo

REMARKS: Other fish species may also be infected. More infected fish are reported during the summer months. Remove parasites if not too numerous and cook fish well. Avoid eating raw fish.

Grunt, sailor's choice *(Haemulon parrai)* *

Miami Seaquarium Photo

LOCATION: Grass beds, reefs, inshore waters.

DISEASE OR CONDITION: Bacterial lesions.

GROSS SIGNS: Red spots on fins and body.

CAUSE: Bacterial infection promoted by sewage pollution.

EFFECT ON MAN: Unappetizing.

---

*This can affect many fish species. See page 36.

REMARKS: It is best not to eat fish from polluted waters, especially near harbors and sewage outfalls. Drainage canals in Florida frequently receive domestic, industrial and agricultural waste. Fish and shellfish taken from these canals may be contaminated.

Mackerel, Spanish mackerel *(Scomberomorus maculatus)*

Photo by F. Berry, NMFS

LOCATION: Open ocean, seasonally in Biscayne Bay.

DISEASE OR CONDITION: Tapeworm infection.

GROSS SIGNS: Long ribbon-like white worm larvae in flesh.

EFFECT ON MAN: Tapeworm larvae ingested with the raw dish "cebiche" have been reported infecting humans in South America and Asia. Mackerel are often used for this dish. No known infections from this area.

REMARKS: Worms are more often found in fish in the summer. Remove parasites. Cook fish well. Accidental infection requires medical attention. Avoid raw fish dishes (cebiche, sashimi, etc.).

Mullet, grey mullet *(Mugil cephalus)*

Miami Seaquarium Photo

LOCATION: Inshore waters.

DISEASE OR CONDITION: Infection with trematodes.

GROSS SIGNS: Small cysts in flesh, eyes, or other organs.

EFFECT ON MAN: Trematode infections of man caused by eating raw fish are well known from Asia. One report from Florida was not substantiated. Symptoms vary according to species ingested and can be serious.

REMARKS: Cook fish well. Avoid raw fish dishes.

Seatrout, spotted seatrout *(Cynoscion nebulosus)*

Miami Seaquarium Photo

LOCATION: Grass beds.

DISEASE OR CONDITION: Tapeworm infection.

GROSS SIGNS: Long ribbon-like white worm larvae in flesh.

EFFECT ON MAN: Some tapeworm larvae can become parasites of man when ingested with raw fish dishes. Reported from Japan and Peru, but no authentic reports from this area.

REMARKS: These worms are more often found in fish in the summer. Clean and cook fish well. Avoid eating raw fish dishes (cebiche, sashimi, etc.), infection requires medical attention.

Snapper, mangrove or grey snapper *(Lutjanus griseus)* *

LOCATION: Inshore, reefs.

DISEASE OR CONDITION: Parasitic infestation with leeches.

---

*And numerous other fish species.

Miami Seaquarium Photo

GROSS SIGNS: Leeches attached to gill area, mouth, or fins.

EFFECT ON MAN: Unappetizing.

REMARKS: Wash fish with fresh water.

Snook *(Centropomus undecimalis)* *

Photo by Jim LaTourrette, Miami Seaquarium

LOCATION: Inshore.

DISEASE OR CONDITION: Parasitic infestation with crustaceans.

GROSS SIGNS: Fish lice on body.

EFFECT ON MAN: Unappetizing.

REMARKS: Wash fish with fresh water before filleting or cleaning.

---

*This condition can occur in numerous other fish species.

Stone crab *(Menippe mercenaria)*

Miami Seaquarium Photo

LOCATION: Inshore areas.

DISEASE OR CONDITION: Trematode infection.

GROSS SIGNS: Dark spots in muscles.

EFFECT ON MAN: Unappetizing.

REMARKS: Parasite is destroyed by cooking.

Stone crab *(Menippe mercenaria)*

LOCATION: Inshore areas.

DISEASE OR CONDITION: Shell disease.

GROSS SIGNS: Discolored, soft, and eroded shell.

CAUSE: Questionable, possibly bacteria.

EFFECT ON MAN: Crab looks unappetizing and the disease probably reduces market value.

REMARKS: Apparently shell disease does not affect the quality of the meat.

Chapter 4.

Some Other Pests: Red Tide, Erysepeloid Bacteria and "Swimmer's Itch"

Several organisms that cause harm to man do not fit into any of the chapters above since they do not really sting, do not bite, or are not poisonous to eat.

Red tide is caused by single celled animals that live free in the water and produce toxins that may poison shellfish that man eats. They may also irritate his skin and the aerosols they produce may irritate his lungs.

"Swimmer's itch" is a free living stage of a fish parasite that can irritate bathers' skin by trying to penetrate it. (Fig. 4). The parasite is actively searching for its normal final host, a bird, and man is attacked.

The bacteria that live on the skin of some fish can irritate any open sore or wound that a person may have. Simply handling the fish can cause this irritation.

"Red tide" *(Gymnodinium breve)*

LOCATION: Coastal waters.

HARM TO MAN: 1. Cause of shellfish poisoning (see page 38). 2. Respiratory irritation. 3. Skin irritation.

CAUSE: Poisonous substance released into the water by minute organisms which appear suddenly in great numbers.

PREVENTION: Find out from the local health authority if it is safe to eat shellfish from the area. Avoid inhaling toxic red tide air. Leave the affected area. Leave the water at first sign of skin irritation from red tide.

AID TO VICTIM: Move victim from the immediate vicinity of the red tide occurrence. In case of shellfish poisoning, seek medical attention.

REMARKS: Causes of "red tide" blooms are still under study.

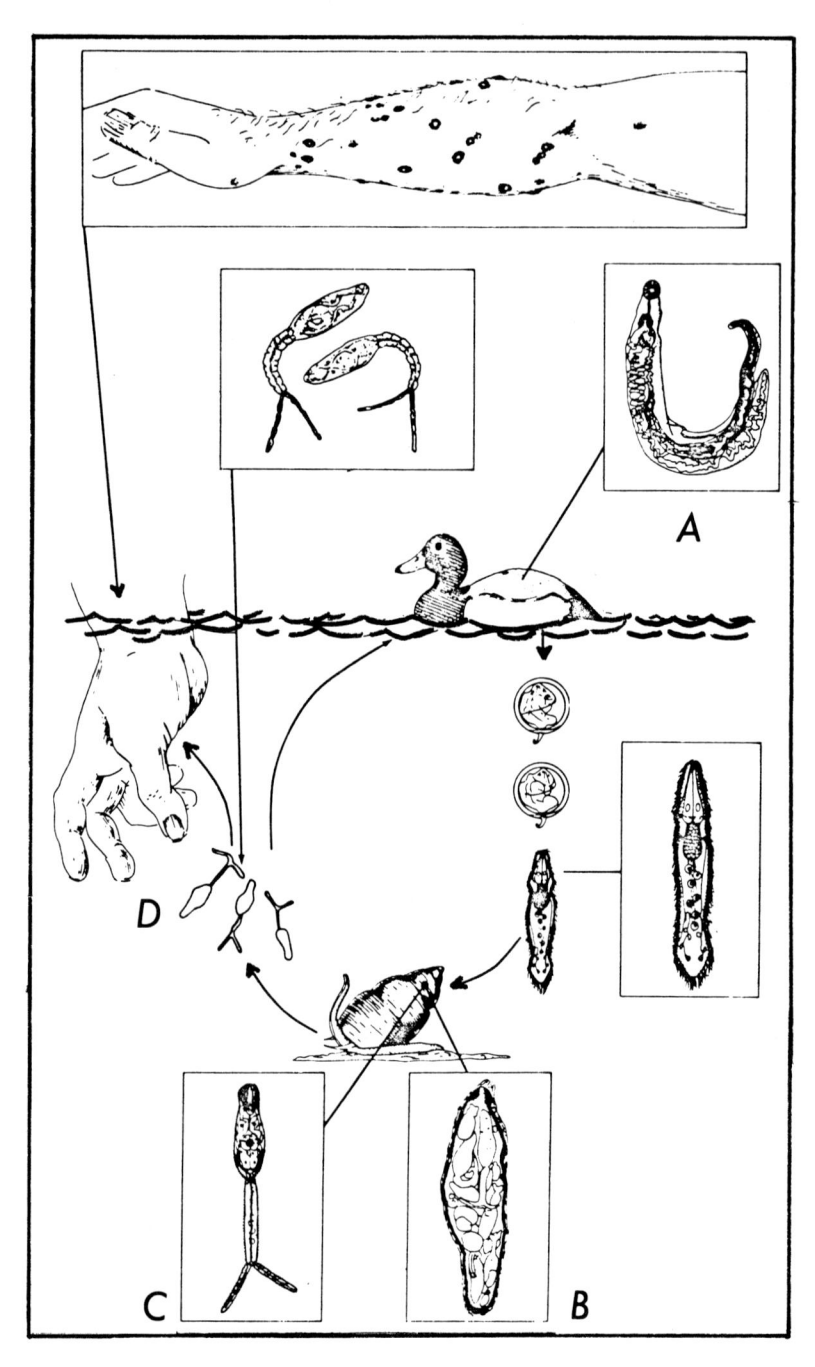

Figure 4. **"Swimmer's Itch."** The trematode parasite, whose normal host is a bird, accidentally penetrates human skin causing a rash or dermatitis. Adult worm (A) in duck sheds eggs that hatch into larval worms (B) and enter snail. Free swimming stage of parasite (C) shed by snail may penetrate human skin. (Based on Sindermann, 1970).

"Swimmer's itch," flatworm larvae *(Austrobilharzia variglandis)*

LOCATION: Beaches, shallow water.

HARM TO MAN: "Swimmer's itch," a skin rash.

CAUSE: Free-swimming flatworm larvae whose normal hosts are birds accidentally penetrate human skin but do not survive in man.

PREVENTION: Do not swim in infested areas, leave the water at first sign of infection.

AID TO VICTIM: Apply alcohol.

REMARKS: A similar dermatitis is caused by blue-green algae which produces a toxic chemical irritating to human skin.

Erysepeloid bacteria

LOCATION: On fish skin.

HARM TO MAN: Inflammation of superficial wounds or injuries.

CAUSE: Wounds become infected with bacteria from the fish.

PREVENTION: Be careful when cleaning fish. Avoid injuries by spines.

AID TO VICTIM: Disinfect wounds.

REMARKS: The bacteria occur naturally on the fish skin and apparently do no harm there.

Chapter 5.
Guidelines

HOW TO AVOID ENDANGERING YOUR HEALTH
A. When wading, bathing, or diving:
   1. Some kind of foot protection should be worn, especially in areas where corals, sea urchins, and sponges grow.
   2. Shuffling your feet reduces the chance of stepping on a spiny or stinging animal.
   3. Do not handle unfamiliar animals, especially fish with spines, jellyfish, or cone-shaped shells. If you do handle these animals, wear gloves.
   4. When diving, do not reach into blind holes or crevices.
   5. Avoid getting scratched by coral, since contamination causes infection and the wound is slow to heal.

6. Avoid areas where large sharks or barracudas might be present. If it is necessary to work in such an area, do not swim alone. If you need help, there will not be any. A wounded shark is frequently more dangerous than a healthy one; do not use a weapon on a shark unless absolutely necessary!

7. Do not carry your catch on your body when spearfishing.

8. Get periodic tetanus shots.

B. When eating seafood.

1. If fish are obtained from an unfamiliar area seek local advice about their edibility. Some areas in the Caribbean are known to have ciguatoxic fish.

2. Avoid eating large fish, especially barracudas, snappers, jacks, and groupers. Fish with beaks (similar to a parrot's beak) eat algae, and should be avoided since they can accumulate poisons.

3. Avoid eating fish taken from waters polluted or suspected of being polluted by human wastes such as waters near sewage outfalls.

4. If there is a question whether a fish that has a good taste is poisonous, eat a very small portion and await results. If, on the other hand, the flesh has a decided "off flavor" or stings the mouth, discard it.

5. Do not eat fish that expand when captured or disturbed, such as puffers and porcupinefish. Do not eat a fish that has no visible scales, like the puffers.

RULES TO FOLLOW IF BITTEN, STUNG OR POISONED

1. If bitten while diving or swimming, and bleeding occurs, leave water at once.

2. Serious wounds need immediate medical attention; minor wounds should be disinfected and given first aid.

3. If venomous stings cause other than localized symptoms, seek medical attention.

4. Severe reactions to poisoning require medical attention or hospitalization.

5. Do not try home remedies on poisoning victim.

6. Do not *delay* seeking medical help when it is indicated.

TREATING STINGS, WOUNDS AND BITES

To clean and disinfect wounds, stings and bites use compounds such as tincture of iodine or 70% alcohol. Sea water is not recommended for washing because it may contain infectious bacteria, especially near shore.

Detailed Symptoms of Fish Poisoning

K.M. Li writing in the Far East Medical Journal Vol. 1, No. 1, 1965, summarizes the symptoms as follows:

CIGUATERA POISONING

"Symptoms and sequence of toxic effects after ingestion of ciguatera fish are similar to those noted after the intoxication from the irreversible types of anticholinesterase drugs such as the organophosphorus nerve gases and agricultural insecticides. There is initial restlessness followed by increased abdominal distress. This is soon succeeded by the appearance of muscle fasciculation, miosis, salivation, lacrimation, sweating, and defecation. The accumulation of bronchial secretions coincides in the respiratory tract with the constriction of the bronchioles, and a stertorous difficult respiration becomes apparent. Tremor, ataxia, and profound weakness develop as a result of central effects and paralysis of the neuromuscular apparatus. The involvement of the respiratory musculature places a further stress on respiration, and dyspnea is an obvious feature. At this point convulsions usually appear and respiration ceases. The heart, although slowed, continues to beat for a period after cessation of respiration. The primary cause of death* is respiratory failure due to peripheral and central consequences of cholinesterase inhibition." **

SCOMBROID POISONING

"Symptoms usually develop within a few minutes to several hours after ingestion and include erythema of the face and upper body; severe occipital headache; giant urticaria; conjunctivitis and periorbital edema; edema of the lips, tongue and throat; respiratory distress; trachycardia; abdominal pain; malaise or generalized weakness and giddiness. Fever and mild diarrhoea may occur as well as nausea, though patients rarely vomit. The acute symptoms usually persist for 8 to 12 hours, after which the patient experiences a rapid recovery; few fatalities have been reported. The treatment recommended is immediate evacuation of the stomach contents, followed by the administration of antihistaminic drugs."

PUFFER POISONING

"Symptoms of poisoning described by various authors may be summarized as follows: Initial symptoms include tingling of the lips, tongue, and fingertips, followed by progression of the numbness which may involve the entire body, and muscular weakness, associated with nausea, vomiting, headache, profuse sweating, hypothermia, and dyspnea. There may be clonic convulsions depending upon the species of mammals and the dose. In severe, acute cases, the patient rapidly develops a weak, rapid pulse, aphonia, marked dyspnea, cyanosis and an ascending paralysis with death resulting from respiratory failure. The mortality rate of persons ingesting toxic puffer fish has been estimated to be greater than 60 percent."

---

*Death occurs in about 7 percent of cases reported (author's note).
**Recent work by Deichmann et al. 1977 suggests that neither ciguatoxin nor ciguaterin are "true" anticholinesterase compounds.

Sources of Information on Dangerous Sea Life in Florida and Adjacent Waters—Research Institutions and Libraries

In addition to the list below, public health, food control or pollution authorities in most cities can be of assistance in locating information on dangerous sea life. Consult your local telephone book.

UNITED STATES

Alabama
University of Alabama
Marine Science Institute
Box 1927
University, Alabama 35486

Florida
Florida Atlantic University
Boca Raton, Florida 33432

Florida State University
Tallahassee, Florida 32306

University of Florida
Center for Aquatic Sciences
Gainesville, Florida 32601

University of South Florida
Marine Science Institute
830 First Street South
St. Petersburg, Florida 33701

University of West Florida
Pensacola, Florida 32504

Florida Institute of Technology
Jensen Beach Campus Library
720 S. Indian River Drive
Jensen Beach, Florida 33457

Harbor Branch Foundation, Inc.
Smithsonian Institution —
    Ft. Pierce Bureau
RFD 1, Box 196
Ft. Pierce, Florida 33450

Florida Institute of Technology
Library
P.O. Box 1150
Melbourne, Florida 32901

Rosenstiel School of
    Marine and Atmospheric Science
University of Miami
4600 Rickenbacker Causeway
Miami, Florida 33149

Southeast Fisheries Center
Fisheries Library, NOAA-NMFS
75 Virginia Beach Drive
Miami, Florida 33149

Florida Department of
    Natural Resources
Marine Research Laboratory
Library
100 Eighth Avenue, SE
St. Petersburg, Florida 33701

Florida Department of
    Natural Resources
Bureau of Coastal Zone Planning
Library
Crown Building, 202 Blount Street
Tallahassee, Florida 32304

University of Miami
Medical School
Coral Gables, Florida 33134

Mote Marine Laboratory
9501 Blind Pass Road
Sarasota, Florida 33581

Georgia
Skidaway Institute of Oceanography
Library
P.O. Box 13406
Savannah, Georgia 31406

Louisiana
Louisiana State University
Department of Marine Sciences
Baton Rouge, Louisiana 70803

Louisiana State University in
 New Orleans
Lake Front
New Orleans, Louisiana 70122

Louisiana Wildlife & Fisheries
P.O. Box 37
Grand Isle, Louisiana 70358

Nicholls State University
Thibodaux, Louisiana 70301

Mississippi
The University of Southern
 Mississippi
Hattiesburg, Mississippi 39401

Gulf Coast Research Laboratory
Ocean Springs, Mississippi 39564

North Carolina
U.S. Department of Commerce
NOAA, National Marine Fisheries
 Service, Atlantic Estuarine
 Fisheries Center Library
Beaufort, North Carolina 28516

University of North Carolina
Zoology Department Library 046-A
Chapel Hill, North Carolina 27514

Biology-Forestry Library
Duke University
Durham, North Carolina 27706

Cape Fear Technical Institute
Library, Learning Resource Center
411 North Front Street
Wilmington, North Carolina 28401

Institute of Marine Sciences
Library
University of North Carolina
P.O. Drawer 809
Morehead City, North Carolina
 28557

Puerto Rico
University of Puerto Rico
Department of Marine Sciences
Mayaguez, Puerto Rico 00708

Inter-American University of Puerto
 Rico
San German, Puerto Rico 00753

Radioecological Division
Puerto Rico Nuclear Center
College Station
Mayaguez, Puerto Rico 00708

South Carolina
South Carolina Marine Resources
 Research Institute
Box 12559
217 Fort Johnson Road
Charleston, South Carolina 29412

Texas
University of Houston
Houston, Texas 77004

Texas A & M University
Marine Laboratory
Building 311, Fort Crockett
Galveston, Texas 77550

Texas Christian University
Fort Worth, Texas 76129

University of Texas at Arlington
Arlington, Texas 76010

University of Texas
Marine Science Institute
Port Aransas, Texas 78373

Gulf Universities Research Corp.
227 System Building
College Station, Texas 77843

The Marine Biomedical Institute
200 University Boulevard
Galveston, Texas 77550

Texas Parks & Wildlife Department
Austin, Texas 78701

Virginia

Virginia Institute of Marine Science
Gloucester Point, Virginia 23062

Old Dominion University Library
Science/Technology Department
5215 Hampton Boulevard
Norfolk, Virginia 23508

U.S. Geological Survey Library
National Center, Mail Stop 950
12201 Sunrise Valley Drive
Reston, Virginia 22092

Washington, D.C.

U.S. Environmental Protection
  Agency, Headquarters Library
Room 2404 Waterside Mall
401 M Street S.W.
Washington, D.C. 20460

U.S. Department of Commerce
NOAA, Page Branch Library
3300 Whitehaven Street, N.W.
Washington, D.C. 20235

U.S. Department of Commerce
NOAA/EDS, Technical Processes
  Branch, National Oceanographic
  Data Center
Washington, D.C. 20235

Smithsonian Institution
U.S. National Museum of Natural
  History
10th and Constitution
Washington, D.C. 20560

U.S. Naval Oceanographic Office
Library (Code 1600)
Washington, D.C. 20373

CARIBBEAN

Bellairs Research Institute
  of McGill University
St. James, Barbados, W.I.

Smithsonian Tropical Research
  Institute
P.O. Box 2072
Balboa, Canal Zone

Instituto Colombo-Aleman
  de Investigaciones Cientificas
Apartado Aereo 1016, Santa Marta
Magdalena, Colombia

Caraibisch Marien – Biologisch
  Instituut
Piscadera Baai
Curaçao, Netherlands Antilles

Instituto de Biologia Marina,
Universidad Autonoma
Santo Domingo
Republica Dominicana

Discovery Bay Laboratory
Discovery Bay, Jamaica

Port Royal Marine Laboratory
University of the West Indies
P.O. Box 12
Kingston 7, Jamaica

Estacion de Investigaciones
  Marinas de Margarita
Fundacion La Salle de Ciencias
  Naturales
Apartado 144, Porlamar
Estado Nueva Esparta, Venezuela

Fundacion Cientifica los Roques
Apartado 61248, Caracas,
Venezuela

Instituto Oceanografico
Universidad de Oriente
Apartado 94
Cumana, Venezuela

Universidad de Zulia
Apartado 1198
Maracaibo, Venezuela

West Indies Laboratory
Fairleigh Dickinson University
P.O. Annex Box 4010
Christiansted, St. Croix
U.S. Virgin Islands 00820

Caribbean Research Institute
College of the Virgin Islands
St. Thomas, V.I. 00801

BAHAMAS
Ministry of Agriculture
 and Fisheries
P.O. Box N-3028
Nassau, N.P., Bahamas

BERMUDA
Bermuda Biological Station
 for Research
St. George's West, Bermuda

CUBA
Universidad de la Habana
Centro de Informacion
 Cientifica y Tecnica
La Habana, Cuba

MEXICO
Instituto Nacional de Pesca
Apartado Postal 184
Ciudad del Carmen
Campeche, Mexico

References

Arnold, Robert E. 1973. *What to Do About Bites and Stings of Venomous Animals* The Macmillan Co., New York, 122 pp.

Bucherl, Wolfgang and Buckley, Eleanor E. 1971. *Venomous Animals and Their Venoms,* Vols. 2 and 3. Academic Press, New York, 687 pp., 560 pp.

Burklew, M. A. and R. A. Morton. 1971. *The Toxicity of Florida Gulf Puffers,* Genus *Sphoeroides.* Toxicon 9:205-210.

Dack, G.M. 1956. *Food Poisoning.* The University of Chicago Press, Chicago, Ill., 251 pp.

Deichmann, Wm. B., W. E. MacDonald, D. A. Cubit, C. E. Wunsch, J. E. Bartels, and F. R. Merritt. 1977. *Pain in Jawbones and Teeth in Ciguatera Intoxications.* Florida Scientist 40(3):227-238.

Gilbert, Perry W. (Editor) 1963. *Sharks and Survival.* D.C. Heath and Co., Boston 578 pp.

Halstead, Bruce W. 1959. *Dangerous Marine Animals.* Cornell Maritime Press, Cambridge, Maryland, 146 pp.

_____. 1965. *Poisonous and Venomous Marine Animals of the World,* Vols. 1, 2, and 3. U.S. Government Printing Office, Washington, D.C.

_____. 1978. *Poisonous and Venomous Marine Animals of the World* (Revised Edition) The Darwin Press, Inc., Princeton, New Jersey. 1043 pp. 283 plates.

Helm, Thomas. 1976. *Dangerous Sea Creatures, a Complete Guide to Hazardous Marine Life.* Funk & Wagnalls. New York. 278 pp.

Holvey, David N., ed. 1972. *The Merck Manual of Diagnosis and Therapy.* Merck, Sharp, and Dohme Research Laboratories, Rahway, New Jersey, 1964 pp.

Hutton, Robert F. 1959. *The Florida Shark Story.* State of Florida Board of Conservation Educational Series No. 13. 37 pp. (Now the Department of Natural Resources).

Morton, R. A. and M.A. Burklew. 1970. *Incidence of Ciguatera in Barracuda from the West Coast of Florida.* Toxicon 8:317-318.

Phillips, C. and W. H. Brady. 1953. *Sea Pests: Poisonous or Harmful Sealife of Florida and the West Indies.* University of Miami Press. 78 pp.

Seaman, William, Jr. 1976. *Sharks and Man: A Perspective.* Conference Proceedings Florida Sea Grant Program. Report Number 10, 37 pp.

Sindermann, Carl J. 1970. *Principal Diseases of Marine Fish and Shellfish.* Academic Press, New York and London, 369 pp.

Sylvester, J. R., A. E. Dammann, and R. A. Dewey. 1977. *Ciguatera in the U. S. Virgin Islands.* Mar. Fish. Review, NOAA, NMFS 39(8):14-16.

Time Life Television. 1976. Wild, Wild World of Animals. Dangerous Sea Creatures. Time Life Television, a Division of Time-Life Films, Inc. Chicago, Ill. 128 pp.

Tsai, Chu-fa. 1975. *Effects of Sewage Treatment Plant Effluents on Fish: A Review of Literature.* Contribution No. 637 Center for Environmental and Estuarine Studies, University of Maryland, 229 pp.

Index

Bold numbers refer to photos.

Acanthurus bahianus 32
alligator 8
Alligator mississippiensis 8
amberjack 22, **22**
anchor worms 40
Arius felis 13
Aurelia aurita 16
Austrobilharzia variglandis 55

bacteria 36, 55
bacteria, erysepeloid 55
Bagre marinus 13
Balistes vetula 34
barbfish 18
barracuda 6, 7, **7**, 23, **23**
biotoxins 38
black drum 46, **46**
blacktip shark 11
blue crab 44, 45, **45**
bluefish 7, 8, **8**, 44, **44**
blue-green algae 55
blue shark 11
blue parrotfish 28, **29**
Bothus lunatus 47
bristle worm 21, **21**

Callinectes sapidus 44, 45
Canthidermis sufflamen 33
Carcharodon carcharias 31
Caranx hippos 26
catfish, gafftopsail 13, **13**
catfish, sea 13, **14**
Centropomus undecimalis 51
cero mackerel 28
ciguatera poisoning 22, 56
conch 23, 24
cone shell 14, **14**
Conus ermineus 14, 15
Conus spurius 14
coral, fire 15, **15**
cowfish, scrawled 20
crab, blue 44, 45, **45**
crab, stone 52, **52**
Crassostrea rhizophorae 38
Crassostrea virginica 37, 38
crevalle jack 26, **27**
crocodile 8, **9**
Crocodylus acutus 8
Cynoscion nebulosus 50

Dasyatis americana 19
Diadema antillarum 18
Diodon hystrix 29

drum, black 46, **46**
drum, striped 46, **46**
drum, red 42

eel 9, **9**, 28, **28**
elasmobranch poisoning 31
Epinephelus striatus 47
Equetus acuminatus 46
Eretmochelys imbricata 35
erysepeloid bacteria 55
Euthynnus pelamis 34

filefish, fringed 24, **24**
fire coral 15, **15**
fire sponge 19, **19**
fish lice 40
fish, reef 39
flatworm 41, 42, **41, 42**
flatworm larvae 40, 42, 55
flounder, peacock 47, **47**

gafftopsail catfish 13, **13**
goatfish, yellow 25
goatfish, spotted 25, **25**
great white shark 11, 31, **31**
great barracuda 6, 7, **7**, 23, **23**
greater amberjack 22, **22**
green moray 28, **28**
grey mullet 49, **49**
grey snapper 32, **32**, 50, **51**
grouper, Nassau 39, **39**, 47, **48**
grubs 42
grunt 39, 48, **48**
Gymnodinium breve 53
Gymnothorax funebris 28
Gymnothorax moringa 9

Haemulon parrai 48
hammerhead shark 11, **11**, 31, **31**
hawksbill turtle 35, **35**
Hermodice carunculata 21
high-hat 46, **46**
hogfish 26, **26**

isopod 41

jack, crevalle 26, **27**
jellyfish 12, 16, **16**

kingfish 27, **27**
king mackerel 27, **27**

Lachnolaimus maximus 26
Lactophrys quadricornis 20
Lactophrys trigonus 20, 34
leeches 40, **41**
lemon shark 11
lice, fish lice 40
Lutjanus griseus 32, 50

63

mackerel 27, **27**, 28, 35, 49, **49**
mackerel, cero 28
mackerel, king 27, **27**
mackerel, Spanish 28, 49, **49**
mako shark 11
mangrove snapper 32, **32**, 50, **51**
man-of-war 16, **17**
Menippe mercenaria 52
Monacanthus ciliatus 24
Millepora 15
moon jellyfish 16, **16**
moray, green 28, **28**
moray, spotted 9, **9**, 10
Mugil cephalus 49
mullet, grey 49, **49**
Mulloidichthys martinicus 25

Nassau grouper 39, **39**, 47, **48**

ocean triggerfish 33, **33**
octopus 10, **10**
Octopus joubini 10
Octopus vulgaris 10
Opsanus tau 11
oyster 37, 38, **38**, **39**
oyster toadfish 11, **12**

parasite cleaners 40
parrot fish 28, **29**
peacock flounder 47, **47**
Pennella 40
pepper spot disease 44
Physalia 12
Physalia physalis 16
Pogonias cromis 46
Pomatomus saltatrix 8, 44
pink conch 23, **24**
porcupinefish 29, **29**
Portuguese man-of-war 12, 16, **17**
Protozoa 40-41
Pseudupeneus maculatus 25
ptomaine 22
puffer 30, **30**
puffer poisoning 22, 57

queen conch 23
queen triggerfish 34

raw fish 43
ray, sting 19, **20**
red drum 42
red sponge 19, **19**
red tide 53
reef fish 39
roundworms 40, 42

sailor's choice 48, **48**
sand tiger shark 11

saltwater crocodile 8
Scarus coeruleus 28
Scomberomorus cavalla 27
Scomberomorus maculatus 49
scombroid poisoning 22, 57
Scorpaena brasiliensis 17
scorpionfish 17, **17**
scrawled cowfish 20
sea catfish 13, **14**
seatrout, spotted 50, **50**
sea urchin 18, **18**
sea wasp 17
Seriola dumerili 22
shark 11, **11**, 31, **31**
shell, cone 14, **14**
shell disease 45, 53
shellfish 6, 36
skipjack tuna 34, **35**
smoked fish 43
snapper, mangrove or grey 32, **32**, 50, **51**
snook 51, **51**
Spanish mackerel 28, 49, **49**
Sphoeroides testudineus 30
Sphyraena barracuda 7, 23
Sphyrna zygaena 6, 31
sponge, fire 19, **19**
spotted goatfish 25, **25**
spotted moray 9, **9**, 10
spotted seatrout 50, **50**
stingray, southern 19, **20**
stone crab 52, **52**
striped drum 46, **46**
Strombus gigas 23
surgeonfish 32, **33**
swimmer's itch **54**, 55

tapeworm **41**
Tedania ignis 19
tiger shark 11
toadfish 11, **12**
trematodes **41**, 54
triggerfish 33, **33**
trout, seatrout 50, **50**
trunkfish 20, **20**, 34, **34**
tuna 34, **35**
turtle, hawksbill 35, **35**

urchin, sea 18, **18**

Vibrio 36

wahoo 28, 35, 42
wasp, sea wasp 17
white shark 11, 31, **31**
worm, bristle 21, **21**
worms, parasitic 40, **41**

yellow goatfish 25